YOUTUBE
S E C R E T
HACKS

INSIDER HACKS FOR SKYROCKETING YOUR

CHANNEL

LUCY MARSHALL

YouTube Secret Hacks

Insider Hacks for Skyrocketing Your Channel

Lucy Marshall

1

Contents

Chapter 1

Introduction to YouTube as a Platform

Welcome to the world of YouTube, where creativity knows no bounds and dreams can become a reality. In this context, we'll discuss on a journey to understand the fascinating landscape of YouTube, exploring its history, its present state, and the incredible potential it offers for individuals like you to make money and carve out a niche in the digital realm.

The Birth of YouTube: A Brief History

YouTube was born in February 2005 when three former PayPal employees, Chad Hurley, Steve Chen, and Jawed Karim, set out to create a platform where anyone could easily share and discover videos online. Little did they know that their brainchild would become a global phenomenon that would redefine the way we consume and create content.

In its early days, YouTube was a platform for sharing personal videos, cat antics, and amateur content. However, it didn't take long for people to recognize its potential for more. The video-sharing platform quickly evolved into a hub for creativity, entertainment, and education.

The Current State of YouTube

Fast forward to the present day, and YouTube has undergone a remarkable transformation. It is now a digital powerhouse with over two billion logged-in monthly users, making it the second-largest search engine after Google. People flock to YouTube not only for entertainment but also for information, education, and inspiration.

YouTube's content landscape is incredibly diverse. You can find everything from makeup tutorials to scientific documentaries, cooking shows to travel vlogs, and everything in between. The platform's popularity spans generations, with content creators ranging from teenagers sharing their passions to seasoned experts sharing their knowledge.

The Power of YouTube: Making Money in the Digital Age

Now, let's delve into the exciting part—making money on YouTube. It's no secret that YouTube has revolutionized the way people earn a living and build careers. The platform offers multiple avenues for monetization, making it an attractive option for aspiring content creators.

Ad Revenue: The YouTube Partner Program

One of the most well-known ways to make money on YouTube is through ad revenue. YouTube's Partner Program allows eligible creators to earn a share of the advertising revenue generated from their videos. The more views and engagement your videos receive, the more money you can potentially earn.

Sponsorships and Brand Partnerships

In the world of influencer marketing, YouTube creators are highly sought after by brands and companies looking to promote their products or services. Collaborating with brands through sponsored videos or partnerships can be a lucrative income stream for YouTubers.

Merchandise and E-commerce

Many successful YouTubers have expanded their revenue streams by selling merchandise related to their channels. T-shirts, mugs, posters, and other branded items can be sold to dedicated fans, creating a direct connection between creators and their audience.

Crowdfunding and Fan Support

Platforms like Patreon allow YouTubers to receive financial support from their loyal fans. Creators can offer exclusive content, perks, and behind-the-scenes access to patrons in exchange for their support.

Affiliate Marketing

YouTubers can earn commissions by promoting products or services through affiliate marketing. When viewers make a purchase through their unique affiliate links, creators receive a percentage of the sale.

Diversification and Beyond

These are just a few of the ways YouTubers can make money, but the possibilities are endless. Some content creators even launch their own businesses, write books, or venture into other creative endeavors outside of YouTube.

As we embark on this journey through the world of YouTube, keep in mind that the platform is not just a place to watch videos; it's a platform where dreams can take flight, where creativity can thrive, and where you have the potential to make a living doing what you love. In the chapters that follow, we'll dive deeper into the strategies, tips, and techniques that will help you unlock your full potential as a YouTuber and harness the power of this incredible platform to achieve your goals. Whether you're an aspiring content creator or an avid YouTube viewer, there's something here for everyone. So, let's get started on the path to success in the world of YouTube.

Chapter 2

Finding Your Niche

In the vast universe of YouTube, finding your niche is akin to locating your guiding star. It's the foundation upon which your YouTube journey will be built. Let us explore the critical process of discovering your niche, a pivotal step towards becoming a successful YouTuber. We'll delve into identifying your interests and expertise, conducting market research, and ultimately selecting a niche that aligns with your passion.

Identifying Your Interests and Expertise

Before you embark on your YouTube journey, it's essential to reflect on your passions and areas of expertise. Your genuine interest in a subject will be your most potent driving force, as creating content can be a labor-intensive endeavor. Here are some steps to help you identify your interests and areas of expertise:

1. Self-Reflection:

Take a moment to consider your hobbies, interests, and the things that genuinely excite you. What activities do you find yourself immersed in when you have free time? What topics do you enjoy discussing with friends and family?

2. Skills and Knowledge:

Think about your professional background, education, and skills. Are there subjects or industries in which you have specialized knowledge or experience? Your expertise can be a valuable asset on YouTube.

3. Passion:

Passion is the driving force behind successful YouTubers. Ask yourself: What would you create content about even if you weren't earning money? What topic would make you excited to get out of bed in the morning?

4. Uniqueness:

Consider what sets you apart from others. Your unique perspective, experiences, or personality can be a significant advantage in attracting and retaining an audience.

Market Research and Audience Analysis

Once you have a list of potential interests and expertise areas, it's time to conduct market research and audience analysis. This step is crucial for understanding the demand for content within your chosen niche and identifying your target audience.

1. Explore Existing Content:

Start by exploring YouTube and other platforms to see what content already exists in your potential niches. Analyze the popular creators in those niches and take note of their content style and audience engagement.

2. Keyword Research:

Utilize tools like Google Keyword Planner and YouTube's search bar to identify relevant keywords and search trends within your potential niches. This will help you understand what people are searching for.

3. Competition Analysis:
Examine your potential competitors. Who are the prominent YouTubers in your chosen niche? What kind of content do they produce? What are their strengths and weaknesses?

4. Audience Persona:
Create a detailed audience persona, including demographics, interests, and pain points. Understanding your target audience will guide your content creation efforts.

Choosing a Niche That Aligns With Your Passion

Now comes the moment of truth—choosing a niche that aligns with both your interests and the potential audience demand. Here's how to make this crucial decision:

1. Passion and Interest:

Select a niche that aligns with your passions and expertise. Remember that your enthusiasm will shine through in your content and engage your audience.

2. Market Demand:

Ensure there is a demand for content in your chosen niche. You want a balance between your passion and the potential audience size.

3. Long-Term Commitment:

Consider whether you can see yourself creating content in this niche for the long term. Building a successful YouTube channel often requires consistent effort over time.

4. Uniqueness:

Identify how you can bring a unique perspective or value to your chosen niche. Being different can help you stand out.

5. Flexibility:

While niching down is essential, allow yourself some flexibility to evolve and adapt as your channel grows. Your interests and audience may evolve over time.

Real-Life Examples

Let's look at a couple of real-life examples to illustrate the process of finding a niche:

- **Example 1: Fitness and Nutrition**

Imagine you're passionate about fitness and nutrition. You have a background in personal training and a genuine desire to help people lead healthier lives. After conducting market research, you discover that there's a significant demand for fitness and nutrition content on YouTube. Many fitness YouTubers have built large followings by providing workout routines, meal plans, and motivational content. This niche aligns perfectly with your passion and expertise.

- **Example 2: Travel and Adventure**

Suppose you have a deep love for travel and adventure. You've explored various destinations, captured breathtaking footage, and have a unique storytelling style. Market research reveals a thriving community of travel enthusiasts on YouTube, and you notice a gap in content that combines adventure with in-depth cultural exploration. This niche not only aligns with your passion but also offers a chance to offer something distinct in the travel content space.

Finding your niche on YouTube is a journey of self-discovery and market exploration. It's about merging your passion and expertise with an understanding of audience demand. Remember that your niche choice will significantly impact your YouTube journey, so take the time to choose wisely. In the chapters that follow, we'll explore how to create high-quality content within your niche, grow your audience, and monetize your channel effectively. So, get ready to turn your passion into a thriving YouTube channel!

Chapter 3

Creating Quality Content

Welcome to the heart of your YouTube journey—creating quality content that captivates your audience, establishes your brand, and sets you on the path to success. In this chapter, we'll delve into the importance of high-quality videos, provide tips for video production, and explore editing and post-production techniques that will elevate your content to the next level.

The Importance of High-Quality Videos

Why is high-quality content so essential on YouTube? Simply put, it's the foundation upon which your channel's success is built. Quality not only attracts viewers but also keeps them coming back for more. Here's why it matters:

1. First Impressions:

Your videos are your first impression on viewers. High-quality content instantly communicates professionalism and competence.

2. Viewer Retention:

Quality content engages viewers and encourages them to watch your videos to the end. This is crucial for YouTube's algorithm and audience growth.

3. Brand Reputation:

Consistently delivering quality content builds your channel's reputation as a reliable source of information or entertainment.

4. Monetization Opportunities:

Brands and sponsors are more likely to collaborate with creators who produce high-quality content. This opens up monetization opportunities.

Tips for Video Production

1. Plan Your Content:

Start by outlining your video's purpose, structure, and key points. Having a clear plan ensures your content is focused and organized.

2. Invest in Equipment:

While you don't need top-of-the-line gear, investing in a good camera, microphone, and lighting equipment can significantly improve video quality.

3. Lighting Matters:

Proper lighting can make a world of difference. Natural light is great, but if not available, invest in softbox lights or ring lights to achieve a professional look.

4. Audio Quality:

Viewers will forgive lower-quality visuals more than poor audio. Invest in a good microphone and record in a quiet environment.

5. Framing and Composition:

Learn the basics of framing and composition. The rule of thirds, leading lines, and proper framing can enhance the visual appeal of your videos.

6. Filming Techniques:

Use a tripod or stabilization equipment to avoid shaky footage. Experiment with camera angles and movements to keep your videos visually engaging.

7. Script and Delivery:

Write a script or outline to stay on track during filming. Practice your delivery to maintain a conversational and engaging tone.

8. B-Roll Footage:

Incorporate B-roll footage to add depth and context to your videos. This can be especially effective in tutorials, vlogs, and travel content.

9. Background and Set Design:

Pay attention to your video's background and set design. A cluttered or distracting background can detract from your content.

10. Consistency:

Maintain a consistent style and branding across your videos. This helps build recognition and trust with your audience.

Editing and Post-Production Techniques

Once you've captured your video footage, the editing and post-production phase is where the magic happens. Here are some key techniques to consider:

1. Video Editing Software:

Invest in professional video editing software like Adobe Premiere Pro, Final Cut Pro, or

DaVinci Resolve. These tools offer advanced editing capabilities.

2. Cut and Trim:

Trim unnecessary footage and eliminate awkward pauses to keep your video concise and engaging.

3. Transitions:

Use smooth transitions between clips to create a cohesive flow. Avoid excessive use of flashy transitions, which can be distracting.

4. Audio Editing:

Clean up audio by removing background noise and adjusting volume levels. Add music or sound effects as needed.

5. Color Correction and Grading:

Enhance your video's colors and mood with color correction and grading. This can make your content visually appealing and consistent.

6. Graphics and Text:

Incorporate graphics, text overlays, and subtitles to provide context and engage viewers.

7. Thumbnail Design:

Create eye-catching thumbnails that accurately represent your video's content. Thumbnails are often the first thing viewers see.

8. Review and Feedback:

Seek feedback from peers or mentors. A fresh perspective can help you identify areas for improvement.

9. Consistency in Style:

Maintain a consistent editing style across your videos. This reinforces your brand and makes your content easily recognizable.

10. Export and Upload:

When exporting your video, use the appropriate settings for YouTube. Optimize file size and quality for online streaming.

Real-Life Examples

Let's look at two real-life examples to illustrate the impact of high-quality video production and editing:

- **Example 1: Travel Vlog**

Imagine you're a travel vlogger exploring the vibrant streets of Tokyo. By investing in quality equipment, mastering framing and composition, and using smooth transitions, your travel vlogs immerse viewers in the beauty and culture of Japan. Your attention to detail in editing, color grading, and thumbnail design makes your content stand out in the crowded travel vlogging niche.

- **Example 2: Educational Channel**

Suppose you run an educational channel teaching complex scientific concepts. Your videos are known for their clear and concise explanations, made possible by meticulous scripting and delivery. You use animations and graphics to simplify concepts further, and your consistent editing style and professional audio quality create a sense of reliability that keeps viewers coming back to learn.

Creating quality content is the backbone of your YouTube channel. It's the bridge that connects you with your audience and sets the stage for growth and success. Whether you're filming travel adventures or educational tutorials, the principles of high-quality video production and editing remain the same. With dedication, practice, and a commitment to improvement, you can produce content that not only meets but exceeds viewer expectations. In the chapters ahead, we'll explore strategies for growing your audience and monetizing your content, but remember, it all starts with delivering exceptional quality.

Chapter 4

Building a Brand and Online Presence

In the dynamic world of YouTube, building a

brand and establishing a strong online presence
are paramount to your success as a content
creator. This chapter will guide you through the
process of creating a memorable channel name
and logo, branding your content and channel,
and the importance of consistency in branding
across platforms. Your brand is not just a logo;
it's the identity that sets you apart in the digital
landscape.

Creating a Memorable Channel Name and Logo

1. Choosing the Right Channel Name:

Your channel name is your digital identity. It should be easy to remember, relevant to your content, and preferably unique. Consider the following when selecting a name:

- Relevance: Ensure your name reflects the niche or theme of your channel. For example, if you're a tech reviewer, a name like "TechInsights" is more relevant than something generic.
- Memorability: Opt for a name that's easy to spell and pronounce. Avoid complicated or obscure words.

- Uniqueness: Check if your chosen name is already in use on YouTube or other platforms to avoid confusion.
- Longevity: Think about whether the name will still make sense as your channel evolves. Avoid overly trendy or time-sensitive names.

2. Designing a Memorable Logo:

Your logo is the visual representation of your channel and brand. It should be simple, distinctive, and easy to recognize. Consider these design principles:

- Simplicity: Keep your logo uncluttered. A clean, straightforward design is more memorable.
- Relevance: Ensure your logo aligns with your channel's theme or niche. If you're a

gaming channel, elements related to gaming can be incorporated.

- Scalability: Design a logo that looks good in various sizes, from a tiny profile picture to a banner.
- Color Palette: Choose a color scheme that complements your brand. Colors evoke emotions, so pick ones that align with your content.
- Typography: If your logo includes text, select a font that's easy to read and consistent with your brand's style.

Branding Your Content and Channel

1. Content Consistency:

Consistency in the type of content you produce is key to building a loyal audience. Your viewers should know what to expect when they visit your channel. Consider:

- Content Style: Maintain a consistent tone and style in your videos. If your channel is known for humor, keep the humor consistent.
- Content Schedule: Stick to a regular posting schedule so viewers anticipate your content. Whether it's weekly or bi-weekly, consistency is key.
- Themes and Series: Create recurring themes or series within your content. This can encourage viewers to binge-watch and stay engaged.

2. Channel Aesthetics:

Your channel's visual aesthetics should align with your brand. This includes your banner, profile picture, and video thumbnails. Consistency in these elements builds recognition:

- Banner: Design a banner that showcases your brand name and captures the essence of your content. It's the first thing viewers see.
- Profile Picture: Use your logo or a clear, high-resolution image of yourself. This helps humanize your channel.
- Thumbnails: Thumbnails should be visually appealing and consistent. Use a template or design elements that tie all your thumbnails together.

3. Branding Elements:

Consider creating branding elements that appear consistently in your videos:

- Intro and Outro: Develop a brief intro and outro that include your logo, channel name, and a call to action.

- Watermarks: Add a subtle watermark of your logo to your videos. It reinforces your brand without being intrusive.

Consistency in Branding Across Platforms

Your YouTube channel is just one piece of your online presence. To maximize your impact, maintain consistency in branding across other social media platforms and your website:

1. Social Media Profiles:
- Use the same profile picture and banner as your YouTube channel.
- Post content related to your channel's niche or behind-the-scenes insights.
- Engage with your audience and respond to comments.

2. Website or Blog:

- If you have a website or blog, ensure its design and content align with your YouTube brand.
- Include links to your social media profiles and YouTube channel.

3. Email Newsletter:

- Consider starting an email newsletter to keep your audience updated on your content and brand developments.

4. Merchandise:

- If you sell merchandise, make sure the branding on your products aligns with your overall brand.

Real-Life Examples

Let's look at two real-life examples of YouTube channels that have successfully built their brand and online presence:

- **Example 1: Tech Reviews Channel**

Imagine a YouTube channel that specializes in in-depth tech reviews. The channel's name, "TechTalk," is straightforward, reflecting its niche. The logo incorporates a sleek, modern design with a tech-inspired color scheme. Video thumbnails consistently feature the same font and style, making them instantly recognizable. The channel maintains a weekly posting schedule and actively engages with its audience on social media platforms.

- **Example 2: Cooking and Lifestyle Channel**

Consider a YouTube channel focused on cooking and lifestyle content. The channel's name, "ChefLife," is memorable and aligns with its theme. The logo includes a playful chef's hat and a warm, inviting color palette. Video thumbnails follow a consistent style, featuring mouthwatering dishes. The channel maintains a cohesive presence on Instagram, sharing behind-the-scenes moments and recipe highlights, all while staying true to its brand.

Building a brand and establishing a strong online presence is a long-term investment in your YouTube career. It's what sets you apart, builds trust with your audience, and creates a lasting impression. Remember that branding is not static; it can evolve as your channel grows. As you embark on your journey to become a successful content creator, commit to creating a brand that resonates with your audience and represents your unique identity. In the upcoming chapters, we'll explore strategies for growing your subscriber base and monetizing your content, but your brand will remain at the core of your YouTube success.

Chapter 5

YouTube SEO and Channel Optimization

In the bustling world of YouTube, getting your

content discovered is a fundamental challenge. To rise above the competition and attract viewers to your videos, you need to understand YouTube's algorithm, master the art of keyword research and optimization, and craft compelling video titles, descriptions, and tags. Welcome to the realm of YouTube SEO and channel optimization, where strategic techniques can significantly boost your visibility and reach.

Understanding YouTube's Algorithm

To excel on YouTube, you must first decipher the mysterious yet powerful entity known as the algorithm. YouTube's algorithm is the behind-the-scenes force that determines which videos are shown to viewers. While YouTube's algorithm is a closely guarded secret, several key factors influence it:

1. Watch Time:

YouTube favors videos that keep viewers engaged. The more time viewers spend watching your content, the better it is for your channel.

2. Click-Through Rate (CTR):

CTR is the percentage of people who click on your video after seeing it in search results or recommendations. A higher CTR suggests that your video is appealing to viewers.

3. Relevance:

YouTube assesses how well your video matches a user's search query or interests. Creating content that aligns with popular and relevant topics is crucial.

4. Engagement:

Comments, likes, shares, and subscribers gained from a video all contribute to its ranking. Engaging content encourages these interactions.

5. Session Time:

YouTube rewards videos that keep viewers on the platform. If your video leads to more extended sessions, it can positively impact your channel's visibility.

Keyword Research and Optimization

Keyword research is the cornerstone of YouTube SEO. By identifying the right keywords, you can optimize your content for search and discoverability. Here's how to master this crucial aspect:

1. Identify Relevant Keywords:

- Use keyword research tools like Google Keyword Planner, Ubersuggest, or YouTube's autocomplete feature to find keywords related to your content.
- Look for keywords with a reasonable search volume and lower competition. Long-tail keywords can be particularly effective.

2. Incorporate Keywords Strategically:

- Place your primary keyword in your video's title. Keep it concise and engaging while including the target keyword.

- Integrate related keywords naturally into your video description and tags. Avoid keyword stuffing, which can have a negative impact.

- Speak the keyword naturally in your video's content. Remember that YouTube's automatic captions can recognize spoken keywords.

3. Monitor Keyword Performance:

- Regularly assess how well your chosen keywords are performing. If some keywords aren't driving traffic, consider revising your strategy.

- Stay updated with trending keywords and adapt your content accordingly.

Crafting Compelling Video Titles, Descriptions, and Tags

Crafting the right video title, description, and tags can be the difference between your video being seen or overlooked. These elements should work together cohesively:

1. Video Titles:

- Make your titles compelling and concise. Clearly convey the video's topic and value.
- Incorporate your primary keyword naturally within the title.
- Consider including emotional or curiosity-driven words to pique interest.

2. Video Descriptions:

- Create detailed and informative descriptions that provide context to your video.
- Begin the description with a brief summary of the video's content.
- Include relevant keywords, but ensure the description reads naturally and offers value to the viewer.
- Add timestamps for key sections of your video to enhance user experience and navigation.
- Include links to related content on your channel or external websites.

3. Video Tags:

- Utilize a mix of broad and specific tags related to your content.
- Place your most important tags first.
- Include common misspellings or variations of keywords.

- Avoid using irrelevant or misleading tags.

4. Thumbnail Relevance:

- Ensure that your video thumbnail aligns with your video's title and description. A cohesive presentation is more likely to attract clicks.

Real-Life Examples

Let's examine two real-life examples to illustrate the impact of YouTube SEO and optimization:

- **Example 1: Travel Vlog - "Exploring Tokyo's Hidden Gems"**

Imagine you run a travel vlog, and one of your videos is about exploring lesser-known attractions in Tokyo. By conducting thorough keyword research, you identify keywords like "Tokyo hidden gems" and "off-the-beaten-path Tokyo." You craft a video title that includes these keywords, such as "Discovering Tokyo's Hidden Gems | Off-the-Beaten-Path Adventures." In your video description, you provide additional information about each location and include timestamps for easy navigation. Your tags include variations of the primary keywords, and your video thumbnail showcases a captivating image from one of the hidden gems. This optimization strategy helps your video rank higher in search results and attract viewers interested in Tokyo travel experiences.

- **Example 2: Tech Review Channel - "Best Budget Smartphones 2023"**

Suppose you operate a tech review channel, and you want to create a video about budget smartphones for the year 2023. After conducting keyword research, you discover keywords like "best budget smartphones 2023" and "affordable phones under $300." Your video title, "Top 5 Budget Smartphones of 2023 | Affordable Phones Under $300," incorporates these keywords. In the video description, you provide detailed specifications and features of each smartphone, along with purchase links. Your tags include variations of the primary keywords, and your video thumbnail displays images of the featured smartphones. This optimization strategy helps your video rank well in search results and attract viewers seeking budget-friendly smartphone recommendations.

YouTube SEO and channel optimization are the cornerstones of content discoverability and audience growth. By understanding the factors that influence YouTube's algorithm, conducting effective keyword research, and crafting compelling video titles, descriptions, and tags, you can significantly enhance your channel's visibility and reach. Keep in mind that SEO is an ongoing process, and staying updated with algorithm changes and trends is essential. In the upcoming chapters, we'll explore strategies for growing your subscriber base and monetizing your content, but a solid foundation in SEO is vital for your YouTube journey.

Chapter 6

Growing Your Subscriber Base

Building a thriving YouTube channel isn't just about creating great content; it's also about fostering a community of loyal subscribers who eagerly anticipate your uploads. In this chapter, we'll explore essential strategies for increasing subscribers, leveraging collaborations and networking to expand your reach, and nurturing an engaged and dedicated audience.

Strategies for Increasing Subscribers

1. Consistent Content Schedule:

Consistency is key to retaining and attracting subscribers. Establish a regular uploading schedule that your audience can rely on. Whether it's weekly, bi-weekly, or monthly, stick to your schedule as closely as possible.

2. Quality Content:

Producing high-quality, valuable content is the most effective way to gain and retain subscribers. Strive to continually improve your content by listening to feedback, staying updated on industry trends, and honing your skills.

3. Audience Engagement:

Interact with your audience in the comments section. Respond to comments, answer questions, and acknowledge your viewers. When your audience feels heard and appreciated, they are more likely to subscribe.

4. Call to Action (CTA):

Incorporate clear and compelling CTAs in your videos. Encourage viewers to subscribe at the beginning or end of your videos. Offer reasons why subscribing would benefit them, such as access to exclusive content or updates.

5. Channel Trailer:

Create an engaging channel trailer that quickly introduces new viewers to your content and the value they can expect. This is often the first impression viewers have of your channel.

6. Use Playlists:

Organize your videos into playlists that make it easy for viewers to binge-watch related content. This can increase the time viewers spend on your channel and encourage them to subscribe.

7. Optimize Thumbnails and Titles:
Craft compelling thumbnails and titles that grab viewers' attention and clearly convey the video's content. A well-designed thumbnail can entice viewers to click and explore more.

8. Cross-Promotion:
Promote your YouTube channel on your other social media platforms, website, or blog. Leverage your existing online presence to attract subscribers to your YouTube channel.

Collaborations and Networking

1. Collaborate with Other YouTubers:

Collaborations are a powerful way to tap into new audiences. Find YouTubers in your niche or related niches and propose collaboration ideas. Collaborative videos can introduce your content to their subscribers and vice versa.

2. Participate in Online Communities:

Join online forums, Facebook groups, or subreddits related to your niche. Engage with the community, share your knowledge, and subtly promote your YouTube channel when relevant. Avoid spamming or self-promotion.

3. Attend Industry Events:

If possible, attend industry events, conferences, or meetups in your niche. Networking with fellow creators and industry professionals can lead to collaboration opportunities and increased visibility.

4. Guest Appearances:

Consider guest appearing on podcasts, webinars, or other YouTube channels. Sharing your expertise or insights on these platforms can help you reach new audiences.

5. Build Relationships:

Focus on building genuine relationships with fellow YouTubers rather than viewing them solely as potential collaborators. Authentic connections can lead to more meaningful partnerships.

Engaging with Your Audience

1. Community Tab:

If your channel is eligible, use the Community tab to interact with your subscribers. Share updates, polls, and behind-the-scenes content to keep your audience engaged.

2. Live Streaming:

Host live streams to connect with your audience in real time. It's an excellent opportunity to answer questions, discuss current topics, and strengthen your bond with subscribers.

3. Q&A Sessions:

Periodically host Q&A sessions where you answer questions submitted by your audience. This can help you better understand their interests and provide valuable content.

4. Audience Feedback:

Actively seek feedback from your audience. Use polls, surveys, or simply ask your viewers what content they'd like to see next. Tailor your content to meet their preferences.

5. Engage on Social Media:

Maintain an active presence on social media platforms where your audience hangs out. Share updates, respond to comments, and engage in conversations related to your niche.

6. Celebrate Milestones:

When you reach subscriber milestones (e.g., 10K, 100K), celebrate with your audience. Host special videos or giveaways to express your gratitude for their support.

Real-Life Examples

Let's explore two real-life examples to illustrate effective subscriber growth strategies:

- **Example 1: Beauty and Makeup Channel**

Imagine you run a beauty and makeup channel. To increase subscribers, you consistently upload tutorials, product reviews, and skincare routines. You actively engage with your audience by responding to comments and featuring viewer-submitted makeup looks in your videos. You collaborate with other beauty YouTubers for makeup challenges and giveaways, tapping into their subscriber base. Additionally, you use your social media presence to share teaser clips and behind-the-scenes content, directing your followers to your YouTube channel.

- **Example 2: Gaming Channel**

Suppose you have a gaming channel where you play and review various video games. To grow your subscriber base, you upload videos on a consistent schedule, focusing on trending and popular games. You actively engage with your viewers during live streams, addressing their questions and reactions. You collaborate with fellow gamers for multiplayer sessions and cross-promote each other's channels. You also participate in gaming forums and Reddit communities, sharing your expertise and subtly promoting your channel when relevant.

Growing your subscriber base is a vital step toward YouTube success. By implementing strategies for increasing subscribers, collaborating with other content creators, and engaging with your audience, you can foster a dedicated and enthusiastic community around your channel. Remember that building a subscriber base takes time and persistence. As you continue on your YouTube journey, focus on providing value to your audience, and your subscriber count will naturally grow. In the chapters ahead, we'll explore monetization strategies and ways to optimize your content for long-term success, but a thriving subscriber base remains the bedrock of your YouTube career.

Chapter 7

Monetization Options

Youtube offers a plethora of opportunities for content creators to turn their passion into a source of income. In this chapter, we'll provide an overview of various revenue streams available on the platform, including ad revenue, sponsored content, merchandise, and more. We'll discuss the pros and cons of each monetization method to help you make informed decisions about how to generate income from your YouTube channel.

Ad Revenue

Overview: Ad revenue is the most common and straightforward way to monetize your YouTube channel. It involves displaying ads on your videos, and you earn money based on factors like ad impressions, clicks, and viewer engagement.

Pros:

1. Passive Income: Once set up, ad revenue generates income passively. You earn money as long as people watch your content.
2. Low Barrier to Entry: You can enable ads on your videos as soon as you meet YouTube's eligibility requirements, including 1,000 subscribers and 4,000 watch hours in the past 12 months.

3. Scalable: As your channel grows and attracts more viewers, your ad revenue potential increases.

Cons:

1. Income Variability: Ad revenue can fluctuate due to factors like ad-blockers, seasonality, and changes in viewer demographics.
2. YouTube's Share: YouTube takes a portion of your ad revenue, typically around 45%, as a service fee.
3. Viewer Experience: Too many ads or intrusive ad formats can annoy viewers and potentially harm your channel's reputation.

Sponsored Content

Overview: Sponsored content involves partnering with brands or companies to create promotional videos or product placements within your videos. You receive payment or free products/services in exchange for featuring them in your content.

Pros:

1. Higher Earnings: Sponsored content often offers higher earnings compared to ad revenue, especially for niche channels with engaged audiences.
2. Creative Freedom: You have creative control over how you incorporate the sponsor's message into your content.
3. Diversified Income: Sponsored content adds diversity to your income sources, reducing reliance on ad revenue alone.

Cons:

1. Disclosure Requirements: You must disclose sponsored content to maintain transparency with your audience.
2. Relevance and Authenticity: Misaligned sponsorships can alienate your audience if they feel the promotion doesn't fit your channel's niche or your personal brand.
3. Finding Partners: Securing sponsorships can be challenging, especially for smaller channels without a substantial following.

Channel Memberships and Super Chats

Overview: Channel Memberships allow viewers to pay a monthly fee to access exclusive perks, such as badges, emojis, or members-only content. Super Chats enable viewers to highlight their messages during live streams by paying a fee.

Pros:

1. Direct Viewer Support: Channel Memberships and Super Chats provide a direct source of income from your most dedicated fans.
2. Engagement Boost: Exclusive perks can incentivize viewers to become channel members and actively participate in live streams.
3. Community Building: These features foster a sense of community among your most loyal supporters.

Cons:

1. Limited to Eligible Channels: Channel Memberships require channel eligibility based on factors like subscriber count and content adherence.

2. Small Percentage of Viewers: Only a fraction of your audience is likely to become paying members or use Super Chats.

3. Content Commitment: To maintain member engagement, you may need to create exclusive content, which can be time-consuming.

Merchandise Sales

Overview: Selling merchandise like t-shirts, mugs, or branded products related to your channel can be a profitable revenue stream. You can use platforms like Teespring or print-on-demand services to create and sell merchandise.

Pros:

1. Brand Promotion: Merchandise serves as a branding tool, increasing your channel's visibility.
2. Creative Expression: You can design merchandise that reflects your channel's personality and resonates with your audience.
3. Profit Margins: You have control over pricing, allowing you to capture a larger portion of the revenue.

Cons:

1. Inventory Management: Handling inventory and order fulfillment can be complex and time-consuming, especially as sales grow.
2. Initial Investment: Designing and producing merchandise may require an upfront investment in design and manufacturing.
3. Market Saturation: Depending on your niche, the market for merchandise may be saturated, making it harder to stand out.

Affiliate Marketing

Overview: Affiliate marketing involves promoting products or services through unique affiliate links. You earn a commission for every sale generated through your links. You can partner with affiliate programs relevant to your content.

Pros:

1. Diverse Opportunities: Affiliate marketing works for a wide range of niches and can be applied to various types of content.
2. Performance-Based: You earn money based on the number of sales or leads you generate, making it directly tied to your content's effectiveness.
3. Passive Earnings: Once you've placed affiliate links in your content, you can earn commissions passively as long as the links remain active.

Cons:

1. Trust and Authenticity: Promoting products solely for commissions can undermine your audience's trust if they perceive it as insincere.

2. Competition: Many affiliate programs have high competition, making it challenging to stand out.

3. Income Variability: Affiliate earnings can vary widely depending on the products or services promoted and the purchasing behavior of your audience.

Crowdfunding and Donations

Overview: Crowdfunding platforms like Patreon and donation features on platforms like PayPal or Ko-fi allow your audience to financially support your channel on a voluntary basis.

Pros:

1. Direct Support: Crowdfunding and donations provide direct financial support from your audience.
2. Freedom: You have control over the incentives and rewards you offer to supporters.
3. Stability: These methods offer a consistent income source, particularly if you have a dedicated fan base.

Cons:

1. Income Reliance: Crowdfunding and donations may not provide a stable income source for newer channels or those with smaller audiences.
2. Incentive Creation: You need to continually provide incentives and exclusive content to retain supporters.

3. Platform Fees: Crowdfunding platforms often charge fees on the contributions you receive.

Real-Life Examples

Let's look at two real-life examples of content creators who effectively utilize multiple monetization methods:

- **Example 1: Tech Review Channel**

Imagine a tech review channel that reviews the latest gadgets and electronics. This channel primarily relies on ad revenue due to its substantial viewership. However, the creator also incorporates affiliate links in video descriptions, earning commissions on product sales. Occasionally, they feature sponsored content, showcasing new products while maintaining transparency with their audience. Additionally, the creator offers Channel Memberships, providing exclusive access to behind-the-scenes content and personalized tech advice.

- **Example 2: Travel Vlog Channel**

Consider a travel vlog channel that documents global adventures. This creator earns income through ad revenue, leveraging their visually appealing content to attract viewers. They also use merchandise sales, selling branded travel apparel and accessories. For direct financial support, the vlogger relies on crowdfunding through Patreon, where subscribers get exclusive access to personalized travel itineraries, travel tips, and early access to videos. The channel also includes affiliate links in their video descriptions, allowing viewers to book accommodations or purchase travel gear, generating additional income.

Monetizing your YouTube channel is not a one-size-fits-all endeavor. By diversifying your income streams and choosing methods that align with your content and audience, you can create a sustainable income from your passion. Keep in mind that the most successful content creators often combine several monetization methods to maximize their earnings. However, authenticity and maintaining trust with your audience should always be at the forefront of your monetization strategies. As you navigate the world of YouTube monetization, remember that patience, dedication, and a focus on delivering value to your viewers are the keys to long-term success. In the upcoming chapters, we'll delve into strategies for optimizing your content and growing your channel further, ensuring that your YouTube journey is both rewarding and profitable.

Chapter 8

Joining the YouTube Partner Program

Monetizing your YouTube channel often begins with becoming a YouTube Partner. This program allows you to earn money from ads displayed on your videos, access additional monetization features, and take steps toward a more profitable channel. In this chapter, we'll cover the eligibility criteria and requirements for joining the YouTube Partner Program, provide a step-by-step guide to becoming a

YouTube Partner, and offer tips for maximizing ad revenue once you're in the program.

Eligibility Criteria and Requirements

Before you can become a YouTube Partner, you must meet certain criteria and adhere to specific guidelines. Here are the key eligibility requirements:

1. YouTube Channel Eligibility:

- Subscriber Threshold: Your channel must have at least 1,000 subscribers.
- Watch Time Threshold: Your channel needs a minimum of 4,000 watch hours in the past 12 months.
- Content Guidelines: Your channel must adhere to YouTube's policies and guidelines, which include copyright compliance and community standards.

2. Monetization Policies:

- Your content must be advertiser-friendly. This means avoiding content that is considered sensitive, controversial, or harmful.
- You must have an AdSense account linked to your YouTube channel.
- Ensure your channel follows YouTube's monetization policies, which include not clicking on your own ads or encouraging others to do so.

3. Geographic Location:

- You must be in a region or country where the YouTube Partner Program is available. YouTube regularly expands its program to cover more regions, so check if your location is eligible.

Step-by-Step Guide to Becoming a YouTube Partner

Becoming a YouTube Partner involves a series of steps to meet the eligibility criteria and complete the application process:

Step 1: Meet the Eligibility Criteria

Ensure your channel has at least 1,000 subscribers and 4,000 watch hours in the past 12 months. Review your content to ensure it complies with YouTube's policies.

Step 2: Sign in to YouTube Studio

Log in to your YouTube channel and access YouTube Studio, where you'll find the "Monetization" tab in the left-hand menu.

Step 3: Agree to the Terms

In the Monetization tab, review and accept the YouTube Partner Program terms and conditions.

Step 4: Set Up an AdSense Account

If you haven't already, set up an AdSense account. You'll need this to receive payments from YouTube. Ensure your AdSense account is linked to your YouTube channel.

Step 5: Enable Monetization

In YouTube Studio, click on "Monetization" and then click "Enable" to activate monetization for your channel.

Step 6: Review and Accept Ad Formats

Select the ad formats you want to enable on your videos. You can choose from various options like display ads, overlay ads, skippable video ads, and more.

Step 7: Wait for Approval

Once you've enabled monetization, YouTube will review your channel to ensure it complies with their policies. This review process can take several weeks, so be patient.

Step 8: Start Earning

Once your channel is approved, you can start earning money from ads displayed on your videos.

Maximizing Ad Revenue

Now that you're a YouTube Partner, you can take steps to maximize your ad revenue:

1. Quality Content: Continue to produce high-quality, engaging content that attracts and retains viewers. Quality content leads to higher ad engagement.

2. Ad Placement: Experiment with ad placement to find what works best for your audience. YouTube allows you to control where ads appear in your videos.

3. Video Length: Longer videos generally have more ad placements and can potentially generate higher ad revenue. However, prioritize content quality over length.

4. Audience Engagement: Encourage viewers to engage with your content, such as liking, commenting, and sharing. High viewer engagement can lead to more ad interactions.

5. Promote Your Videos: Use social media and other promotional methods to increase your video views. More views mean more opportunities for ads to be shown.

6. Analyze Analytics: Regularly review your YouTube Analytics to understand your audience's behavior and preferences. Use this data to refine your content and ad strategy.

7. Diversify Monetization: In addition to ad revenue, explore other monetization methods like sponsored content, merchandise sales, and affiliate marketing to supplement your income.

8. Stay Compliant: Continuously adhere to YouTube's policies and guidelines. Any violations can result in limited monetization or channel penalties.

9. Engage with Your Audience: Keep your audience engaged by responding to comments, hosting live streams, and building a community around your channel.

10. Experiment and Adapt: The YouTube landscape is constantly evolving. Stay updated with industry trends and adapt your content and monetization strategies accordingly.

Becoming a YouTube Partner is a significant milestone in your YouTube journey, opening doors to various monetization opportunities. By meeting the eligibility criteria, following the application process, and adhering to YouTube's policies, you can start earning money from ads displayed on your videos. However, ad revenue is just one aspect of monetization, and diversifying your income sources can lead to a more stable and profitable channel. As you progress, remember that providing value to your audience remains the core of your YouTube success, and monetization should enhance, not compromise, your content's quality and authenticity. In the following chapters, we'll explore advanced strategies for channel growth and content optimization to help you thrive as a YouTube creator.

Chapter 9

Brand Partnerships and Sponsorships

Brand partnerships and sponsorships are

lucrative opportunities for YouTubers to

monetize their channels while collaborating

with companies and brands. In this context,

we'll delve into the strategies for finding and

approaching potential sponsors, negotiating

sponsorship deals, and maintaining good

relationships with brands to create successful

and long-lasting partnerships.

Finding and Approaching Potential Sponsors

1. Understand Your Niche and Audience:

- Identify the specific niche or category your channel falls under. Knowing your niche is essential for targeting relevant sponsors.
- Understand your audience demographics, interests, and preferences. Sponsors are more likely to partner with creators who have an audience aligned with their target market.

2. Create a Compelling Media Kit:

- Develop a professional media kit that includes key information about your channel, such as your audience demographics, reach, engagement metrics, and past collaborations.

- Showcase your channel's strengths, unique selling points, and the benefits of partnering with you.

3. Utilize Influencer Marketing Platforms:

- Join influencer marketing platforms like AspireIQ, GrapeVine, or Famebit. These platforms connect content creators with brands looking for partnerships.
- Set up your profile, highlight your channel's strengths, and apply for relevant sponsorship opportunities.

4. Identify Brands in Your Niche:

- Research brands that operate in your niche or have products/services relevant to your content. Make a list of potential sponsors.

- Follow these brands on social media, engage with their content, and familiarize yourself with their marketing campaigns.

5. Engage in Industry Events and Conferences:

- Attend industry-related events, conferences, and trade shows. These gatherings offer opportunities to network with brand representatives and discuss potential collaborations.
- Exchange business cards, introduce yourself, and express your interest in working together.

6. Approach Brands with a Personalized Pitch:

- Craft a personalized pitch for each brand you're interested in partnering with.

Highlight how your channel can benefit their marketing goals and reach their target audience.

- Be concise and compelling in your pitch. Brands receive numerous sponsorship requests, so make yours stand out.

Negotiating Sponsorship Deals

1. Determine Your Worth:

- Assess the value you bring to the partnership. Factors like your audience size, engagement rates, and niche relevance play a role in determining your worth.

- Research industry standards and pricing benchmarks to get a sense of what sponsors typically pay for similar collaborations.

2. Clarify Expectations:

- Clearly define the scope of work, deliverables, and expectations for both parties. This includes the type of content you'll create, posting schedule, and any additional promotional activities.
- Address key details such as compensation, content ownership, and usage rights.

3. Negotiate Compensation:

- Negotiate compensation that reflects your channel's value and the effort required for the partnership. Compensation can include monetary payment, free products, or a combination of both.
- Be prepared to provide a breakdown of your pricing and the benefits the brand will receive.

4. Set Milestones and Deadlines:

- Establish clear milestones and deadlines for the partnership. This ensures that both you and the brand stay on track and meet expectations.
- Include timeframes for content creation, review, and publication.

5. Draft a Detailed Agreement:

- Create a formal sponsorship agreement that outlines all terms and conditions. This agreement should cover compensation, deliverables, content rights, exclusivity clauses, and dispute resolution mechanisms.
- Consider consulting a legal professional or using contract templates to ensure clarity and legality.

6. Maintain Open Communication:

- Maintain open and transparent communication with the brand throughout the partnership. Address any concerns or issues promptly and professionally.
- Share progress updates, seek feedback, and ensure alignment with the brand's objectives.

Maintaining Good Relationships with Brands

1. Deliver Quality Content:

- Fulfill your partnership obligations by creating high-quality content that aligns with the brand's messaging and resonates with your audience.
- Exceed expectations whenever possible to build trust and long-term relationships.

2. Meet Deadlines:

- Adhere to agreed-upon timelines and deadlines for content creation and publication. Timely delivery reflects professionalism and reliability.

3. Promote the Sponsorship:

- Actively promote the sponsored content on your channel and social media platforms. Encourage your audience to engage with the brand's content and products.
- Show your commitment to the partnership by going beyond the basic requirements.

4. Report on Results:

- Provide the brand with performance analytics and results of the sponsored content. Share data on engagement, views, click-through rates, and audience feedback.

- Demonstrate the impact of the partnership on their marketing goals.

5. Seek Feedback and Improvement:

- After the collaboration, ask for feedback from the brand. Understand what worked well and where improvements can be made.

- Use this feedback to enhance future partnerships and refine your approach.

6. Express Gratitude:

- Express appreciation and gratitude to the brand for the partnership opportunity. A thank-you note or gesture of gratitude can leave a positive impression.

- Consider sending a follow-up message expressing your interest in future collaborations.

Real-Life Example

Let's explore a real-life example of a successful brand partnership:

Example: Cooking Channel Collaboration with a Kitchen Appliance Brand

Imagine you run a cooking channel on YouTube, specializing in quick and easy recipes. A well-known kitchen appliance brand approaches you for a collaboration to promote their new blender.

Approach:

You research the brand and the blender to ensure it aligns with your channel's cooking theme. You draft a personalized pitch outlining how you can create engaging recipe videos featuring the blender. You emphasize your channel's 500,000 subscribers, high engagement rates, and previous successful collaborations with food-related brands.

Negotiation:

In negotiations, you discuss compensation, which includes a monetary payment and a complimentary blender. You agree to create three recipe videos showcasing the blender's versatility, with a posting schedule over three weeks. Both parties agree on content ownership and usage rights.

Partnership Execution:

You create visually appealing recipe videos, incorporating the blender into the cooking process. You publish the videos as scheduled and actively promote them on your social media channels. You also host a giveaway where your viewers can win the same blender, increasing audience engagement.

Results and Follow-Up:

The sponsored videos receive high views and positive comments from your audience. You provide the brand with detailed analytics, including click-through rates and increased brand visibility. The brand expresses satisfaction with the partnership, and you express gratitude for the opportunity.

Brand partnerships and sponsorships can be mutually beneficial relationships that provide YouTubers with income and brands with exposure to their target audience. By following the strategies for finding sponsors, negotiating deals, and maintaining good relationships, you can create successful and lasting partnerships. Keep in mind that authenticity, professionalism, and delivering value to both your audience and the brand are key to building trust and fostering long-term collaborations. As you continue to grow your channel and explore sponsorship opportunities, remember that each partnership is an opportunity to enhance

Chapter 10

Creating and Selling Merchandise

Merchandise sales offer YouTubers an exciting opportunity to monetize their channel while deepening connections with their audience. Here, we'll navigate the process of designing and producing merchandise, integrating a merchandise store with your channel, and effective marketing and promotion strategies to boost merchandise sales.

Designing and Producing Merchandise

1. Understand Your Audience:

- Start by understanding your audience's preferences. What kind of merchandise would resonate with them? Consider their age, interests, and the themes of your channel.

2. Develop Unique Designs:

- Create original and compelling designs that reflect your channel's identity and resonate with your audience. Consider collaborating with a graphic designer if you're not proficient in design.
- Ensure that your designs are clear, visually appealing, and scalable to different merchandise items.

3. Select Merchandise Items:

- Decide which merchandise items you want to offer. Common options include t-shirts, hoodies, mugs, posters, phone cases, and stickers.
- Consider the production cost, pricing, and potential profit margins for each item.

4. Choose a Printing and Fulfillment Method:

- Decide whether you'll print and fulfill merchandise orders yourself or use a print-on-demand service. Print-on-demand services handle production, shipping, and customer service, which can be more convenient for creators.
- Research and select a reputable printing and fulfillment partner.

5. Quality Control:

- Ensure that the merchandise items meet your quality standards. Order samples to assess the print quality, material, and overall finish.

6. Set Pricing:

- Determine the pricing for each merchandise item. Consider factors like production costs, desired profit margins, and what your audience is willing to pay.
- Be competitive but avoid underpricing your merchandise.

Integrating a Merchandise Store with Your Channel

1. Create an Online Store:

- Set up an online store on an e-commerce platform that aligns with your preferences. Popular options include Shopify, WooCommerce (for WordPress users), and Printful.
- Customize your store to reflect your channel's branding and aesthetics.

2. Integrate with Your YouTube Channel:

- Link your merchandise store to your YouTube channel. You can do this by adding a link to your store in your video descriptions, channel banner, or the merchandise shelf (if eligible).
- Prominently feature merchandise links in your video descriptions and encourage viewers to check out your store.

3. Provide Detailed Product Descriptions:

- Write clear and compelling product descriptions for each merchandise item. Include information about sizing, materials, and care instructions.
- Use persuasive language to highlight the unique selling points of your merchandise.

4. Optimize for Mobile:

- Ensure that your merchandise store is mobile-friendly. Many viewers access YouTube and make purchases on mobile devices.
- Test the user experience on mobile devices to ensure a seamless shopping process.

5. Offer Variety and Limited-Edition Items:

- Keep your merchandise store fresh by periodically introducing new designs or limited-edition items. This creates a sense of urgency and encourages repeat purchases.
- Consider themed merchandise related to special milestones or events on your channel.

Marketing and Promoting Your Merchandise

1. Promote in Your Videos:

- Actively promote your merchandise in your YouTube videos. Mention it during your intros or outros and explain the value of your merchandise to your audience.

- Showcase merchandise items by wearing or using them in your videos.

2. Host Giveaways:

- Host merchandise giveaways to generate excitement and engagement. Encourage viewers to participate by subscribing, liking, and sharing your videos.
- Announce winners in a video or on social media to build anticipation.

3. Leverage Social Media:

- Utilize your social media platforms, such as Instagram, Twitter, and Facebook, to showcase your merchandise. Share high-quality images and videos of your merchandise items.

- Use relevant hashtags and engage with your audience through posts, stories, and live sessions.

4. Collaborate with Other Creators:

- Collaborate with fellow YouTubers or influencers to cross-promote each other's merchandise. This can expose your merchandise to new audiences.
- Feature other creators wearing or using your merchandise in your videos.

5. Create FOMO (Fear of Missing Out):

- Implement scarcity marketing tactics by highlighting limited quantities or limited-time offers for certain merchandise items.
- Encourage viewers to act quickly to avoid missing out on exclusive items.

6. Offer Bundles and Discounts:

- Create merchandise bundles that offer a discount when multiple items are purchased together. This encourages larger orders.

- Periodically offer discounts or promotions to incentivize purchases.

7. Engage with Customer Feedback:

- Encourage customers to leave reviews and provide feedback on their merchandise purchases. Positive reviews can build trust with potential buyers.

- Address any customer concerns or issues promptly and professionally.

Real-Life Example

Let's explore a real-life example of a successful merchandise strategy:

- **Example: Gaming   Channel Merchandise**

Imagine you run a popular gaming channel on YouTube. You decide to launch a merchandise line featuring designs related to your channel's branding and gaming themes.

Design and Production:

You collaborate with a professional graphic designer to create eye-catching and unique designs. You choose a print-on-demand service to handle production and fulfillment, ensuring high-quality printing on t-shirts, posters, and mugs.

Integration with Your Channel:

You set up an online merchandise store using Shopify and link it to your YouTube channel. You add merchandise links in your video descriptions and mention your store in your video outros.

Marketing and Promotion:

In your videos, you wear merchandise items and highlight their quality and design. You announce merchandise giveaways in your videos and on social media, driving engagement and excitement.

You actively engage with your gaming community on social media, using gaming-related hashtags to reach a broader audience. Collaborations with other gaming

YouTubers include cross-promotion of each other's merchandise.

You periodically run limited-time promotions, such as "holiday bundles" and "limited-edition collector's items," creating a sense of urgency and exclusivity.

Customer Engagement:

You encourage buyers to leave reviews and share photos of themselves wearing or using your merchandise on social media. You acknowledge and thank customers for their support, fostering a sense of community around your merchandise.

Creating and selling merchandise can be a rewarding addition to your YouTube channel's revenue streams. By designing appealing merchandise, integrating your store with your channel, and effectively marketing and promoting your products, you can monetize your content while strengthening your connection with your audience. Put it in mind that the success of your merchandise venture depends on delivering quality products that resonate with your viewers and providing exceptional customer service. As you continue to grow your channel, your merchandise can become a valuable part of your overall brand and revenue strategy.

Chapter 11

Diversifying Income Streams

Diversifying your income streams as a YouTuber is a key strategy for financial stability and growth. Over Reliance on ad revenue can be risky, given its variability and the evolving YouTube landscape. Here, we'll explore additional income sources, including Patreon, affiliate marketing, and digital products, and discuss how to reduce reliance on ad revenue.

Exploring Additional Income Sources

1. Patreon:

- What is Patreon: Patreon is a platform that allows content creators to receive ongoing financial support from their audience, known as "patrons." Patrons pledge a monthly amount to support their favorite creators.

- How It Works: You can set up a Patreon page and offer different tiers of rewards or benefits to your patrons. These rewards can include exclusive content, early access, behind-the-scenes updates, or personalized interactions.

- Benefits: Patreon provides a consistent source of income that is not reliant on ad revenue fluctuations. It fosters a closer connection with your most dedicated fans and encourages long-term support.

2. Affiliate Marketing:

- What is Affiliate Marketing: Affiliate marketing involves promoting products or services through unique affiliate links. You earn a commission for every sale or lead generated through your affiliate links.
- How It Works: Join affiliate programs relevant to your niche or content. Incorporate affiliate links in your video descriptions or blog posts, and disclose that you may earn a commission.
- Benefits: Affiliate marketing diversifies your income by providing a performance-based revenue stream. You can partner with brands you genuinely support and leverage your audience's trust.

3. Digital Products:

- What are Digital Products: Digital products include e-books, online courses, templates, presets, or any digital content you can sell to your audience.
- How It Works: Create valuable digital products related to your niche or expertise. Promote and sell these products through your YouTube channel and other online platforms.
- Benefits: Selling digital products allows you to leverage your knowledge and expertise to generate income. It provides scalable revenue with minimal production costs once created.

Reducing Reliance on Ad Revenue

1. Set Realistic Ad Revenue Expectations:
- Understand that ad revenue may not be substantial, especially for smaller

channels. It often takes time to build a substantial viewership.

- Avoid relying solely on ad revenue as your primary income source, especially in the initial stages of your YouTube journey.

2. Diversify from Day One:

- Start diversifying your income streams from the beginning. Explore options like affiliate marketing and merchandise sales early in your channel's development.
- Building multiple income sources takes time, so the earlier you start, the better.

3. Invest in High-Quality Content:

- Focus on creating high-quality, engaging content that attracts and retains viewers. High-quality content can lead to more subscribers and better opportunities for monetization.

- Quality content is more appealing to potential sponsors, patrons, and customers.

4. Regularly Assess and Adjust:

- Periodically evaluate the performance of your income streams. Identify which sources are most profitable and which need improvement.
- Adjust your strategies based on the performance data and changing audience preferences.

5. Balance Monetization with Audience Experience:

- Prioritize delivering value to your audience over aggressive monetization.

Maintaining a positive viewer experience can lead to long-term growth and loyalty.

- Avoid overwhelming your content with ads or promotions that may alienate your audience.

6. Plan for Financial Stability:

- Aim to build a financial cushion that can support your content creation efforts during periods of lower ad revenue or unexpected challenges.
- Having savings or other income sources can alleviate financial stress.

Real-Life Example

Let's look at a real-life example of a YouTuber who effectively diversified their income streams:

- **Example: Lifestyle Vlogger**

Imagine you run a lifestyle vlogging channel, sharing content related to travel, health, and personal development.

Diversification Strategies:

- Patreon: You create a Patreon page where you offer exclusive travel tips, behind-the-scenes vlogs, and personalized health advice to your patrons. This provides a consistent monthly income stream from your most dedicated viewers.
- Affiliate Marketing: You partner with travel and wellness companies and include affiliate links in your video descriptions. When viewers book vacations or purchase health products

through your links, you earn commissions.

- Digital Products: You create an ebook about maintaining a healthy lifestyle while traveling and an online course on mindfulness and well-being. You promote these digital products in your videos and sell them on your website.

Results:

- Your Patreon community grows steadily, providing a stable income source that supports your travel expenses and content production.
- Affiliate marketing generates commissions from travel bookings and health product sales, increasing your monthly earnings.

- The sales of your ebook and online course bring in additional revenue, and you continually update and expand your digital product offerings.

Diversifying your income streams as a YouTuber is a strategic move to reduce reliance on ad revenue and build a more stable and profitable channel. Exploring options like Patreon, affiliate marketing, and digital products can provide consistent income sources that complement ad revenue. Never forget that the key to success is balancing monetization with audience satisfaction and providing value to your viewers. As you continue to grow your channel and expand your income sources, your financial stability and creative freedom will increase, allowing you to focus on what you love—creating content that resonates with your audience.

Chapter 12

Managing Finances and Taxes

Managing finances and understanding the

tax implications of your YouTube income is crucial for financial stability and compliance with the law. In this context, we'll explore how to track income and expenses, important tax considerations for YouTubers, and the benefits of working with financial professionals.

Tracking Income and Expenses

1. Separate Business and Personal Accounts:

- Open a dedicated business bank account for your YouTube earnings and related expenses. This separation simplifies financial management and tax reporting.

2. Record All Income:

- Keep meticulous records of all your income sources, including ad revenue, sponsorships, merchandise sales, affiliate marketing earnings, and Patreon contributions.
- Utilize accounting software or spreadsheets to track income, making it easier to calculate total earnings.

3. Expense Tracking:

- Maintain detailed records of business-related expenses, such as equipment purchases, software subscriptions, travel expenses for content creation, and any fees associated with running your channel.
- Categorize expenses for better organization and analysis.

4. Regular Reconciliation:

- Periodically reconcile your income and expenses to ensure accuracy. This process helps identify discrepancies and ensures you have a clear financial picture.

5. Budgeting:

- Create a budget that outlines your expected income and expenses. This helps you plan for financial stability and set aside funds for taxes.

- Monitor your actual spending against your budget and make adjustments as needed.

Tax Considerations for YouTubers

1. Tax Classification:

- Determine the appropriate tax classification for your YouTube income. Many YouTubers operate as sole proprietors, but other options include forming an LLC or corporation.
- Consult a tax professional or legal advisor to determine the best structure for your specific situation.

2. Income Reporting:

- Report all income, including ad revenue, sponsorships, and merchandise sales, on your tax return. Failure to report income can result in penalties.
- Keep copies of tax forms provided by platforms like YouTube, affiliate marketing programs, and merchandise sales platforms.

3. Deductions:

- Identify and claim eligible deductions for your YouTube business. Deductions can include expenses related to equipment, software, home office space, travel, and marketing.
- Consult a tax professional to ensure you maximize your deductions while staying compliant with tax laws.

4. Quarterly Estimated Taxes:

- If you expect to owe a significant amount in taxes, consider making quarterly estimated tax payments to the IRS. This prevents a large tax bill at year-end and potential penalties.

5. Self-Employment Tax:

- YouTubers are typically considered self-employed and are subject to self-employment tax, which covers Social Security and Medicare contributions.
- Be prepared to set aside funds for self-employment tax in addition to income tax.

6. Tax Credits and Deductions:

- Explore tax credits and deductions that may apply to your situation. For example, the home office deduction or education-related tax credits for courses that enhance your skills.

- Stay informed about changes in tax laws that may affect YouTubers.

Working with Financial Professionals

1. Accountant or Tax Advisor:

- Consider hiring an accountant or tax advisor with experience in self-employment and creative industries. They can help you navigate complex tax regulations, identify deductions, and ensure compliance.
- An accountant can also provide guidance on quarterly tax payments and assist with tax planning.

2. Financial Planner:

- A financial planner can help you create a financial plan that includes savings, investments, and retirement planning. They can help you set financial goals and make informed decisions about your YouTube income.
- Look for a Certified Financial Planner (CFP) or Certified Public Accountant (CPA) with expertise in working with self-employed individuals.

3. Legal Advisor:

- If you're considering forming an LLC or corporation, consult with a legal advisor to understand the legal and tax implications of your business structure.
- They can assist with the necessary paperwork and ensure compliance with state and federal regulations.

4. Bookkeeper:

- If you find it challenging to manage your finances and keep accurate records, consider hiring a bookkeeper. They can handle day-to-day financial transactions and maintain organized records.

- This can free up your time to focus on content creation and growing your channel.

Real-Life Example

Let's explore a real-life example of a YouTuber who benefited from working with financial professionals:

- **Example: Tech Reviewer**

Imagine you run a YouTube channel where you review and test various tech products, and you earn income from ad revenue, sponsorships, and affiliate marketing.

Financial Professionals Involved:

- Accountant: You hire a CPA with experience in self-employment and digital content creation. They help you categorize your income and expenses, identify deductions, and estimate quarterly tax payments.
- Financial Planner: You consult with a financial planner to create a retirement savings plan and investment strategy. They help you allocate a portion of your income toward long-term financial goals.

Results:

- Your accountant ensures that you accurately report your income and claim all eligible deductions, resulting in reduced tax liability.
- With guidance from your financial planner, you establish a retirement account and investment portfolio, allowing you to build wealth and secure your financial future.
- Both professionals help you achieve financial stability while navigating the complexities of self-employment taxes.

Managing your finances and understanding tax considerations is vital for the long-term success of your YouTube career. By tracking income and expenses, adhering to tax regulations, and working with financial professionals, you can ensure financial stability, reduce tax liabilities, and make informed decisions about your income and investments. Put it in mind that financial management is an ongoing process, and staying organized and informed is key to a successful YouTube business. As you continue to grow your channel and income, financial planning and compliance become even more critical for your success and peace of mind.

Chapter 13

Handling Copyright and Legal Issues

Navigating copyright and legal matters is an essential aspect of running a YouTube channel. In this context, we'll delve into copyright infringement and fair use, protecting your content, and dealing with potential legal challenges.

Copyright Infringement and Fair Use

1. Copyright Basics:

- Copyright law grants creators exclusive rights to their original works, including videos, music, and images, as soon as they're created and fixed in a tangible form.
- Unauthorized use or reproduction of copyrighted content is considered copyright infringement and can lead to legal consequences.

2. Fair Use Doctrine:

- Fair use is a legal doctrine that allows limited use of copyrighted material without permission from or payment to the copyright holder under certain circumstances, such as for commentary, criticism, news reporting, teaching, or research.
- Fair use is determined on a case-by-case basis, considering factors like the

purpose of use, the nature of the copyrighted work, the amount used, and the effect on the market for the original work.

3. Avoiding Copyright Infringement:

- Always seek permission or a license when using copyrighted material in your videos. This applies to music, images, video clips, and any content that you didn't create yourself.
- Use royalty-free music, public domain content, or material licensed under Creative Commons when possible.

4. Attribution and Credit:

- When using others' content with permission, provide proper attribution as required by the licensing terms.

- Properly credit the creators of any third-party content you use, even if it falls under fair use.

5. YouTube's Copyright Policies:

- Familiarize yourself with YouTube's copyright policies and the Content ID system. Content ID scans videos for copyrighted material and may place restrictions or monetization claims on videos that contain copyrighted content.
- Understand how to dispute copyright claims and resolve disputes through YouTube's tools.

Protecting Your Content

1. Utilize Copyright Protection Tools:

- Enable YouTube's Content ID system to automatically detect and manage the use of your copyrighted content by others.
- Register your original work with the U.S. Copyright Office to gain additional legal protections.

2. Watermarking and Branding:

- Watermark your videos with your channel logo or name. This helps establish your ownership and deters potential copyright infringers.
- Incorporate your branding into your content to make it easily recognizable as your intellectual property.

3. Terms of Use and Licensing:

- Clearly outline your terms of use and licensing for your content. Specify how others can use your videos, whether for personal use, commercial use, or with attribution.

- Consider using Creative Commons licenses if you want to allow certain uses while retaining control over others.

Dealing with Legal Challenges

1. Responding to Copyright Claims:

- If you receive a legitimate copyright claim on your video, consider whether it's valid. If it's not, dispute the claim through YouTube's system with supporting evidence.
- Be prepared to negotiate with copyright holders and potentially reach a resolution, such as removing the disputed content or providing proper attribution.

2. Seek Legal Advice:

- If you're facing complex legal challenges related to copyright, fair use, or defamation, consult an attorney with expertise in intellectual property or media law.
- Legal professionals can provide guidance and representation if needed.

3. Defamation and Privacy Concerns:

- Understand defamation laws and privacy considerations when creating content that involves individuals or organizations.
- Avoid making false statements that could harm someone's reputation, and respect individuals' privacy rights.

4. Review YouTube's Policies:

- Regularly review and adhere to YouTube's community guidelines and policies to ensure your content complies with platform rules.
- Familiarize yourself with YouTube's process for handling legal complaints and takedown requests.

Real-Life Example

Let's look at a real-life example of how a YouTuber handled a copyright dispute:

- **Example: Travel Vlogger**

Imagine you run a travel vlogging channel where you showcase your adventures around the world. In one of your videos, you used a short clip of a popular song while featuring a beautiful beach scene.

Challenge:

The music label that owns the song filed a copyright claim on your video, resulting in monetization going to the label instead of your channel.

Response:

1. Assess the Claim: You reviewed the copyright claim and determined that it was valid since you had used the song without permission.
2. Dispute the Claim: You disputed the claim through YouTube's system, acknowledging that the claim was valid but explaining that you used the music for artistic purposes and that it fell under fair use.

3. Resolution: The music label reviewed your dispute and agreed to release the claim, allowing your video to be monetized again. You credited the song in your video description to provide proper attribution.

Handling copyright and legal issues is a critical aspect of maintaining a successful YouTube channel. Understanding copyright laws, respecting fair use principles, and protecting your own content are essential steps to avoid legal disputes. In cases where legal challenges arise, it's important to respond appropriately, whether by disputing a copyright claim, seeking legal advice, or making necessary adjustments to your content. By staying informed and following best practices, you can create a channel that not only entertains and informs but also operates within the bounds of the law.

Chapter 14

Staying Current and Adapting to Changes

Staying current and adapting to changes on

the YouTube platform is crucial for long-term

success as a content creator. Here, we'll explore

the impact of YouTube algorithm updates,

trends and shifts on the platform, and strategies

for maintaining relevance and growth.

YouTube Algorithm Updates

1. Understanding the Algorithm:

- The YouTube algorithm plays a central role in determining which videos are recommended to users. It considers factors like watch time, user engagement, video metadata (titles, descriptions, tags), and viewer history.
- Regularly stay informed about YouTube's algorithm updates and how they may impact your channel's visibility and reach.

2. Quality and Engagement:

- Focus on creating high-quality content that engages your audience. High watch time, likes, comments, and shares are key signals that the algorithm uses to promote videos.
- Encourage viewers to interact with your content by asking questions, running polls, or hosting contests.

3. Consistency and Frequency:

- Consistency in uploading content can improve your channel's performance. Stick to a regular posting schedule that aligns with your audience's expectations.

- Balance frequency with quality to ensure you don't sacrifice content quality for the sake of posting more frequently.

4. Audience Retention:

- Keep viewers engaged throughout your videos. Monitor your audience retention metrics to identify where viewers tend to drop off and work on improving those segments.

- Use compelling intros, clear storytelling, and engaging visuals to maintain viewer interest.

5. Keyword Research:

- Stay updated on relevant keywords and topics within your niche. Use tools like Google Trends, YouTube's search suggest feature, and keyword research tools to identify trending topics.
- Incorporate relevant keywords naturally into your video titles, descriptions, and tags.

Trends and Shifts in the Platform

1. Changing Viewer Behavior:

- Pay attention to shifts in viewer behavior, such as the rise of mobile viewing, shorter attention spans, and changing content consumption patterns.
- Adapt your content and presentation style to align with these changes.

2. Emerging Content Formats:

- Stay aware of emerging content formats and trends on YouTube. These may include short-form content, live streaming, vertical videos, or interactive experiences like YouTube Shorts.
- Experiment with new formats to see what resonates with your audience.

3. Platform Features and Tools:

- Regularly explore and utilize new features and tools offered by YouTube. These can include community posts, YouTube Stories, merch shelf, and YouTube Premiere.
- Experimenting with these features can help you engage with your audience in unique ways.

4. Competition and Collaboration:

- Keep an eye on your competitors and channels within your niche. Observe their strategies and content to identify successful approaches.

- Consider collaborations with other creators to tap into new audiences and fresh ideas.

Strategies for Long-Term Success

1. Diversify Content:

- Don't rely solely on one type of content. Diversify your content to appeal to a broader audience and adapt to changing trends.

- For example, if you primarily create tutorials, consider incorporating vlogs or opinion pieces to add variety to your channel.

2. Community Building:

- Foster a sense of community among your viewers. Engage with comments, host live chats, and respond to audience feedback.
- Building a loyal fan base can provide stability and support during platform changes.

3. Data Analysis:

- Regularly analyze your channel's performance data. Monitor audience demographics, traffic sources, and watch time trends.
- Use data-driven insights to refine your content strategy and adapt to audience preferences.

4. Adaptability:

- Be open to change and willing to adapt your content strategy as needed. What worked in the past may not always work in the future.
- Experiment with new approaches and be prepared to pivot when necessary.

5. Long-Term Goals:

- Set long-term goals for your channel. These goals can include subscriber milestones, revenue targets, or expanding into new content niches.
- Having a clear vision for the future helps guide your content creation efforts.

6. Continued Learning:

- Stay curious and committed to learning. Follow industry news, attend YouTube conferences, and engage with online communities of creators.

- Learning from others and staying updated on best practices is essential for growth.

Real-Life Example

Let's explore a real-life example of a YouTuber who adapted to changes and trends on the platform:

- **Example: Educational Channel**

Imagine you run an educational YouTube channel that teaches programming and coding skills. Over the years, you've witnessed changes in viewer behavior, with more viewers accessing content on mobile devices.

Adaptation Strategy:

1. Mobile-First Content: You recognized the shift toward mobile viewing and started creating shorter, more concise coding tutorials optimized for mobile screens.

2. Interactive Quizzes: To engage your audience further, you introduced interactive quizzes within your videos using YouTube's interactive card feature. This encouraged viewers to participate and test their knowledge.

3. Community Engagement: You fostered a community of aspiring programmers by hosting weekly live Q&A sessions where viewers could ask questions and receive real-time guidance.

4. Content Diversification: While your core content remained coding tutorials, you occasionally created opinion pieces on

industry trends and the future of programming, broadening your content portfolio.

5. Data-Driven Insights: You consistently analyzed audience retention data and viewer comments to identify areas for improvement and create content that aligned with audience preferences.

Results:

- Your adaptability to changing trends and audience behavior led to increased engagement and subscriber growth on your channel.
- The mobile-friendly content and interactive quizzes resonated with viewers, resulting in higher watch time

and a boost in algorithm recommendations.

- Your community engagement efforts helped build a loyal following, with viewers eagerly awaiting your live Q&A sessions.

The YouTube platform is dynamic, and staying current and adapting to changes are essential for long-term success. By understanding the YouTube algorithm, keeping up with platform trends, and employing adaptable strategies, you can maintain relevance and continue to grow your channel. Never forget that success on YouTube often requires a combination of creativity, data analysis, community building, and a willingness to evolve with the ever-changing digital landscape. As you navigate the challenges and opportunities of the platform, your ability to adapt and innovate will be key drivers of your channel's success and longevity.

Chapter 15

Success Stories and Case Studies

In this final chapter, we'll delve into the inspiring success stories and case studies of notable YouTubers who have achieved remarkable accomplishments on the platform. By exploring their journeys, lessons learned, and the inspiration they provide, aspiring YouTubers can glean valuable insights and motivation for their own YouTube endeavors.

1. PewDiePie: From Bedroom to Billions

Profile: Felix Kjellberg, better known as PewDiePie, is one of the most recognized and successful YouTubers globally, known for his gaming and commentary content.

Key Lessons:

- Consistency is Key: PewDiePie posted videos regularly, maintaining a consistent upload schedule, even when his channel was small. This consistency helped build his audience over time.
- Authenticity Matters: PewDiePie's genuine personality and unfiltered reactions resonated with viewers. Authenticity can be a powerful magnet for a loyal fan base.
- Adapt and Evolve: PewDiePie didn't limit himself to one type of content. He adapted to changing trends and expanded his content to include challenges, vlogs, and more.

Inspiration: PewDiePie's journey from a bedroom YouTuber to a global sensation demonstrates that dedication, authenticity, and adaptability can lead to extraordinary success on the platform.

2. Nas Daily: Telling Stories that Matter

Profile: Nuseir Yassin, the creator behind Nas Daily, is known for his one-minute daily vlogs that showcase unique stories from around the world.

Key Lessons:

- Unique Value Proposition: Nas Daily found a niche by creating concise, meaningful content that distinguished him from other vloggers.

- Storytelling Mastery: He excels at storytelling, turning everyday moments into compelling narratives. Storytelling is a powerful tool for engagement.
- Global Connection: Nas Daily's content fosters a sense of global community, bringing people together through shared experiences and stories.

Inspiration: Nas Daily's success demonstrates that a clear value proposition, exceptional storytelling, and a global perspective can resonate with audiences and create a positive impact.

3. Emma Chamberlain: Authenticity and Relatability

Profile: Emma Chamberlain is a lifestyle vlogger and influencer known for her relatable and unfiltered content.

Key Lessons:

- Embrace Imperfection: Emma's willingness to show her imperfections and be vulnerable on camera makes her highly relatable to her audience.
- Unique Voice: She developed a unique and relatable style that stood out in the saturated vlogging space.
- Community Building: Emma engages with her audience authentically, creating a tight-knit community of fans who feel like they know her personally.

Inspiration: Emma Chamberlain's journey illustrates that being yourself, embracing authenticity, and connecting with your audience on a personal level can lead to substantial success as a YouTuber.

4. Mark Rober: Combining Passion and Expertise

Profile: Mark Rober, a former NASA engineer, creates educational and entertaining science-related content.

Key Lessons:

- Leverage Expertise: Mark combined his engineering background with his passion for education to create engaging science experiments and explanations.

- Value-Driven Content: He focused on delivering educational value while keeping the content entertaining, making science accessible to a broader audience.
- Consistency and Patience: Mark's channel grew gradually over time, emphasizing the importance of patience and a long-term perspective.

Inspiration: Mark Rober's story demonstrates how blending expertise with passion and a commitment to educational value can lead to success while making learning enjoyable.

5. MrBeast: Impact Through Generosity

Profile: MrBeast, also known as Jimmy Donaldson, is known for his philanthropic and entertaining videos, often involving extreme challenges and generous giveaways.

Key Lessons:

- Dare to Be Different: MrBeast carved a unique niche by combining extreme challenges with philanthropy, creating content that stands out.
- Giving Back: His generosity and willingness to give away large sums of money earned him a dedicated fan base and media attention.
- Pushing Limits: MrBeast's willingness to take risks and attempt ambitious challenges sets him apart from other creators.

Inspiration: MrBeast's journey showcases how creativity, generosity, and a willingness to push the boundaries of content creation can lead to both personal fulfillment and a massive following.

6. Casey Neistat: Master of Storytelling

Profile: Casey Neistat is a filmmaker and vlogger known for his cinematic storytelling and visually stunning videos.

Key Lessons:

- Storytelling Craft: Casey's background as a filmmaker and his dedication to storytelling sets his content apart. He often uses cinematic techniques in his vlogs.
- Consistency and Quality: He combines a regular posting schedule with a commitment to producing high-quality content.

- Personal Brand: Casey's strong personal brand and unique style have earned him a devoted following.

Inspiration: Casey Neistat's journey underscores the power of storytelling and the impact of maintaining consistent quality in your content.

Conclusion

These success stories and case studies of prominent YouTubers provide valuable insights and inspiration for aspiring creators. While their journeys differ in many ways, several common themes emerge:

- Authenticity: Being true to oneself and embracing imperfections can resonate deeply with an audience.
- Creativity: Thinking outside the box and daring to be different can set your content apart from the crowd.
- Consistency: Maintaining a consistent posting schedule and content quality is key to building an audience over time.
- Engagement: Engaging with your audience and fostering a sense of community can create a loyal fan base.
- Value: Providing educational or entertaining value to your viewers is at the heart of successful content.

Never forget that success on YouTube is not defined solely by numbers but by the impact you make and the fulfillment you derive from your content creation journey. By learning from these case studies and applying their lessons to your own YouTube endeavors, you can chart a path toward achieving your unique goals and making your mark on the platform.